Pupil Book 1

Vocabulary, Grammar and Punctuation

Author: Abigail Steel

William Collins' dream of knowledge for all began with the publication of his first book in 1819. A self-educated mill worker, he not only enriched millions of lives, but also founded a flourishing publishing house. Today, staying true to this spirit, Collins books are packed with inspiration, innovation and practical expertise. They place you at the centre of a world of possibility and give you exactly what you need to explore it.

Collins. Freedom to teach.

Published by Collins
An imprint of HarperCollins*Publishers*
The News Building
1 London Bridge Street
London
SE1 9GF

Browse the complete Collins catalogue at
www.collins.co.uk

© HarperCollins*Publishers* Limited 2015

10 9 8 7 6 5 4 3 2 1

ISBN 978-0-00-813336-8

British Library Cataloguing in Publication Data
A Catalogue record for this publication is available from the British Library

Edited by Hannah Hirst-Dunton
Cover design and artwork by Amparo Barrera
Internal design concept by Amparo Barrera
Typesetting by Jouve India Private Ltd
Illustrations by Jacqui Davis, Aptara and QBS

Printed in Italy by Grafica Veneta S.p.A.

Contents

Adding -s and -es

When we want to show that there is more than one of something, we use the endings **-s** or **-es**. Endings like this are called **suffixes**. We use **-es** if the word for the single thing ends in the letters **ch**, **sh**, **s**, **x** or **z**.

- One **cat**   Two **cat<u>s</u>**
- One **fox**   Two **fox<u>es</u>**

Get started

Copy the sentences. Underline the suffixes **-s** and **-es**. One has been done for you.

1. My cats are black.

Answer: My cat<u>s</u> are black.

2. We pack the boxes.

3. I saw some chicks in a nest.

4. Look at those pink buses!

5. The children sat on the benches.

Try these

Copy and correct these sentences. You need to add the suffix **-s** or **-es** to the underlined words. One has been done for you.

1. I put my <u>sock</u> on my feet.

   Answer: *I put my <u>socks</u> on my feet.*

2. I have three paint <u>brush</u>.

3. All my <u>pen</u> had run out.

4. The <u>fox</u> were in the den.

5. I had six <u>book</u>.

Now try these

Add the suffix **-s** or **-es** to each word. Then use it in a sentence of your own.

1. gift

2. wish

Adding endings to root words (-ing,-ed, -er, -est)

We can change words by adding the endings **-ing**, **-ed**, **-er** or **-est**. Endings like this are called **suffixes**.

- The farm**er** was milk**ing** his cow.
- I wait**ed** for the slow**est** bus.

Get started

Copy the sentences. Underline the suffixes **-ing**, **-ed**, **-er** and **-est**. One has been done for you.

1. I added one extra sweet to the bag.

   Answer: *I add<u>ed</u> one extra sweet to the bag.*

2. Max is a teacher in the next town.

3. Samir needed to finish his task.

4. Zak is the fastest boy in the race.

5. Dad was sleeping in his chair.

Try these

Copy and correct these sentences. You need to add the suffix **-ing**, **-ed**, **-er** or **-est** to the underlined words. One has been done for you.

1. I was **<u>meet</u>** my pet for the first time.

   Answer: *I was <u>meeting</u> my pet for the first time.*

2. The **<u>garden</u>** has green fingers.

3. Dad **<u>paint</u>** the wall.

4. Katya is **<u>look</u>** at her book.

5. Raj is the **<u>loud</u>** singer.

Now try these

Add the suffix **-ing** to each word. Then use it in a sentence of your own.

1. paint

2. play

Adding the prefix un-

We can make a word mean its **opposite** by adding the letters **un-** to the beginning. Added beginnings like this are called **prefixes**.

- Kit is **un**fair to her sister Pat.

- Pat can not **un**lock the car to get in.

Get started

Copy the sentences. Underline the prefix **un-**. One has been done for you.

1. Tom can not undo the box.

   Answer: *Tom can not <u>un</u>do the box.*

2. Karam will unhook the gate for you.

3. Meena is unafraid of bugs.

4. Jen will unload her bags.

5. Marc did some unpaid jobs.

Try these

Copy and correct these sentences. You need to add the prefix **un-** to the underlined words. One has been done for you.

1. The <u>lit</u> room was dark.

    Answer: *The <u>unlit</u> room was dark.*

2. Eva can not <u>stick</u> her teeth from the toffee!

3. Jayden will <u>block</u> the sink for us.

4. When I go to bed, I <u>dress</u> myself.

5. Dad is <u>fit</u> as he likes burgers too much!

Now try these

Add the prefix **un-** to each word. Then use it in a sentence of your own.

1. fair

2. pack

Building sentences

We can make a sentence when we put words together in the correct order. A sentence needs a capital letter at the start and a full stop at the end.

- Sam sits on the mat.
- The ducks swim on the pond.

Get started

Put the words in order to make a sentence. One has been done for you.

1. barking. The dog is

    Answer: *The dog is barking.*

2. pin drops. The

3. jam. Marvis likes

4. Tim ball. the has

5. at look him. We

Try these

Copy and complete each sentence using one word from the box. The sentence should make sense! One has been done for you.

1. The fox ____ in the wood.

runs / cats

Answer: *The fox <u>runs</u> in the wood.*

2. The little ____ dig down.

3. Sam is ____ the bath.

4. The sun is so _____.

5. I have socks on my _____.

have / bugs
they / in
moon / hot
feet / you

Now try these

1. Write one sentence about your lunch. Use a capital letter at the start and use a full stop at the end. Check your sentence makes sense.

2. Write one sentence about your family. Use a capital letter at the start and use a full stop at the end. Check your sentence makes sense.

Building sentences using 'and'

We can join two short sentences together with the linking word **and**. This makes two sentences into one longer sentence.

- She likes books **and** she likes maps.
- The sun is up **and** he is hot.

Get started

Copy the sentences. Underline the word **and**. One has been done for you.

1. She brushes her hair and she brushes her teeth.

Answer: *She brushes her hair <u>and</u> she brushes her teeth.*

2. I can hop and you can jump.

3. I like bats and he likes hats.

4. I can swim and we can sail.

5. Jaz will sing and he will shout.

Try these

Copy the sentences. Add **and** to join them. One has been done for you.

1. I can stomp _____ and you can stamp.

Answer: *I can stomp <u>and</u> you can stamp.*

2. She hears bells _____ she hears horns.

3. I go to you _____ you come to me.

4. It is raining _____ we get wet.

5. It is winter _____ you have a chill.

Now try these

Put the words in the correct order to make sentences.

1. flowers   We   see   bees   see we   and   .

2. swinging   running   He   likes she   likes   and   .

Punctuating sentences

Sentences always need a capital letter at the start.
At the end you need to put a full stop, a question mark
or an exclamation mark.

- Full stop: **.**

- Statement: I am nine.

- Question mark: **?**

- Question: Are you glad?

- Exclamation mark: **!**

- Exclamation: She is so funny!

Get started

Copy the sentences. Underline the capital letters. Then draw a
ring around the end punctuation. One has been done for you.

1. Jamal went for a run.

   Answer: <u>J</u>amal went for a run⊙

2. Jan had a trip and fell!

3. There was a black bird in the garden.

4. What did my cat do?

5. My cat sat on a car.

Try these

Copy the sentences. Draw a ring around the full stops. Underline the question marks once. Underline the exclamation marks twice. One has been done for you.

1. I went to see a film.

    Answer: *I went to see a film⊙*

2. What was it like?

3. It was good.

4. What happened in it?

5. There was a funny clown!

Now try these

Copy the sentences. Add the capital letters and pick the correct end punctuation.

1. can you skip

2. i like books

3. a shark is in my pond

Capital letter for names and 'I'

We use a capital letter at the start of a name and for the word **I** when we write about ourselves. We still use a capital letter at the start of a sentence.

- We went to the shop with **P**olly.
- Can **I** have a glass of milk?

Get started

Copy the sentences. Underline the capital letters. One has been done for you.

1. *We got the book for Mark.*
2. She did art with Jorge.
3. After this, I will go swimming.
4. Then I can see Kim.
5. Jon and I did maths with Klaus.

Try these

Copy the sentences. You need to add capital letters. One has been done for you.

1. now carol has a doll.

   Answer: _Now_ _Carol_ has a doll.

2. it is a fact that i like frogs.

3. did you see how eva can run?

4. mum said that i sing like a pop star.

5. the cat is called matt.

Now try these

1. Write three names, using capital letters.

2. Write three words that do not need a capital letter.

Capital letter for days of the week and place names

We use a capital letter at the start of place names and the days of the week.

We still use a capital letter at the start of a sentence, for names and for the word **I** when we write about ourselves.

- On **S**unday we have a tennis match.
- Then **I** will go to **M**anchester.

Get started

Copy the sentences. Underline the capital letters. One has been done for you.

1. I live in Liverpool.

   Answer: <u>I</u> live in <u>L</u>iverpool.

2. We got the bus to London.

3. I went to Oxford.

4. We will have fun on Sunday.

5. On Monday we will be in the town of Bognor.

Try these

Copy the sentences. You need to add capital letters. One has been done for you.

1. i think robin lives in ashford.

Answer: *I think Robin lives in Ashford.*

2. we have a big day on tuesday.

3. it is a fact that friday is the day after thursday.

4. the town of elgin is in scotland.

5. we go to paris on saturday.

Now try these

1. Write three place names, using capital letters.

2. Write two sentences to introduce yourself and where you live, using capital letters.

For example: *I am Anna. I live in Oxford.*